BLOGGING

How To Make Money Online And Build Your Own $100,000+ Online Business Blogging

Anthony Paker

Copyright © 2018 Anthony Paker

It is not legal to reproduce, duplicate, or transmit any part of this document in either electronic means or in printed format. Recording of this publication is strictly prohibited.

ISBN:1987550099
ISBN-13:9781987550092

CONTENTS

Introduction i

Chapter One: Can You Make Money Blogging?..... 1

Chapter Two: Choosing The Right Niche 8

Chapter Three: Choosing The Right Name For Your Blog 20

Chapter Four: Setting Up Your Blog 30

Chapter Five: Creating A Content Strategy For Your Blog............ 47

Chapter Six: Building Traffic.. 62

Chapter Seven: Turn Your Audience Into Revenue...................... 81

Chapter Eight: Eight Common Mistakes To Avoid 105

Final Words 118

Introduction

Thank you for purchasing this book!

There have been many stories recently of people making millions of dollars through blogging, allowing them to live a life of true freedom, with the ability to work from anywhere in the world. This kind of lifestyle probably sounds alluring, and you might be wondering if it possible for you to do the same, to create your own blog that rakes in over $100,000 a year. Well, you can! Anyone can build a profitable blog and make tons of money online.

Many of the people who attempt to build a profitable blogging business do not succeed. This is because most people do not take the right approach to blogging. Most treat blogging as a hobby instead of approaching it as a business. This book will show you the right blogging approach that will allow you to build a profitable blogging business that brings in thousands of dollars per month.

Whether you're looking to supplement your income with some extra money to pay for a few nice treats or looking to completely support your lifestyle by blogging, this book will teach you everything you need to know. It doesn't matter if you are completely new to blogging; the information contained in this book will teach you how to build your own blog from scratch and how to turn it into a money-making machine.

Are you ready to kick-start your blogging career? Let's jump in!.

Chapter One: Can You Make Money Blogging?

One of the most common questions that people who are thinking of starting a blog have is: "Can someone really make good money from blogging?"

This question is not entirely baseless. On one hand, there's a lot of hype around the topic of blogging. There are several people who have made claims of how they were able to make millions from their blogs in a very short time. On the other hand, there are people who claim that it is impossible to make a decent living from blogging. So, which group is correct? The reality, as it usually does, lies somewhere between the claims of the two groups.

Currently, there are millions of live blogs in the world, but most do not bring in any significant income for their owners. At the same time, there are rock-star bloggers who make a killing every month. The difference between the successful bloggers who make millions from their blogs and the rest of the pack lies in their approach to blogging. Successful bloggers approach their blog not as a hobby, but as a business. They treat themselves as entrepreneurs trying to build a business from scratch. They understand that, just like with a traditional brick-and-mortar business, building a profitable blog takes time, lots of trial and error, and lots of learning. They also understand that there is always the risk of failure. With the right approach, however, anyone can make money through blogging.

Before we get into the specifics of how to make money through blogging, there are a number of things I want to make clear about building a profitable blog:

1. It Is Possible

Making money through blogging is very possible. I know this from experience. I have launched several blogs, most of which have gone on to bring in substantial incomes. What you need to understand is that you won't create a blog today and hit the million-dollar mark tomorrow. Your blog will start by bringing in a few dollars a day at most. However, if you continue doing everything the right way, your income will gradually grow to significant levels. This means that you should not quit your job so that you can start a blog. Instead, at the very start, you should treat your blog as a part-time job. As it grows and starts bringing in decent income, you can then make your blog a full-time job. It can even grow into a fully-fledged business that employs others.

2. There's No Magic Method For Making Money From A Blog

There are several ways of monetizing a blog. Some bloggers will make money by selling eBooks, while others will make money by being coaches, while still others will make money by promoting their offline business. This means that as a blogger, you should not be rigid to one method of income generation. Instead, you should be open to experimentation. Try different methods of monetization and find one that works best for you. In fact, the highest-earning bloggers do not depend on any one method of income generation. Instead, they have multiple streams of income from the same blog. I will discuss different methods of monetization in greater detail later in the book.

3. There Are Many Profitable Niches

If you read about the topic of monetizing a blog, you will find "experts" claiming that there are only a few niches in which money can be made. This is simply not true. There are lots of profitable niches. If you do a research on the highest-earning bloggers, you will realize that they are from varied niches. These include niches like passive income, food, travel, parenting, photography, fashion, hair, crafts, dating, design, and so on. The list is endless. These niches are not even related, yet people have been able to make money through all of them. However, this does not mean that you should jump into whatever niche comes across your mind. Instead, you should do your research and determine if there's potential in a niche before getting into it. In the next chapter, I will discuss in greater detail the process of identifying a profitable niche.

4. It Takes Time

Blogging is not a get-rich-quick scheme. Before you can start earning from your blog, you need to build an audience, build a brand, and cultivate trust with your audience. All these things take time. If you look at bloggers in the top income bracket, you will realize that most of them have been blogging for three years or more. Therefore, you should be ready to put in lots of work with little or no returns at the start of your blogging journey.

5. It Takes A Lot Of Work

Many people selling the hype of making money from blogging present it as a passive method of income generation. However, from my own experience, I know that nothing could be farther from the truth. Blogging requires lots of hard work, especially at the beginning. Creating great content on a regular basis is a lot of work.

Promoting your content to generate traffic is a lot of work. Creating products to sell, monitoring the business side of things and keeping abreast of trends in the blogosphere is a lot of work. If you want to build a profitable blog, you should be ready to do all this. It won't be easy, but if you choose a niche that you are passionate about, it will be fun and enjoyable.

So, the answer to the question asked at the beginning of this chapter is that it is indeed possible to make money through blogging. There are several different niches and monetization methods for doing this. However, you should understand that it is not easy. It takes time and a lot of hard work. However, if you follow the right steps and do everything that is included in this book, you will definitely be able to build a profitable blog.

Chapter Summary

- It is possible for anyone to make money through blogging.

- There are several ways through which you can make money from your blog.
- There is no shortage of profitable niches.
- It takes time to build a profitable blog.
- You will need to put in a lot of hard work before you can start generating a significant income from your blog.

In the next chapter, you will learn how to pick the right niche for your blog.

Chapter Two: Choosing The Right Niche

In this chapter, you are going to learn how to choose the right niche to blog about.

One of the biggest problems most aspiring bloggers grapple with is deciding what to write about. Actually, this is one of the most important decisions you will make when starting your blog. It is a major determinant of your blog's success or failure, and therefore, you need to ensure that you get it right.

It is important that you blog about a specific topic. If you decide to blog about everything under the sun, you will never run out of content. However, it will be very hard for you to build recurrent targeted traffic, and even harder for you to make money off your blog. This is why you will notice that the most popular and successful blogs identify themselves around one of these categories:

- A specific niche
- A specific demographic
- A particular challenge people have

So, how do you choose a niche that you should blog about? If you look this up on the internet, you will notice that nearly every resource mentions three things: passion, traffic, and profitability.

Well, this makes sense. If you don't have passion, chances are that you will abandon your blog before you even start making money. You might write for a couple months and run out of steam. In these cases, you need passion to keep you going. However, I believe that people can be passionate about anything that is going to make them some money. Plus, you could be passionate about a number of things. Should you blog about all your passions? Probably not.

Traffic is important, because you don't want to create a blog that will only be read by your friends and family.

Choosing a niche with high traffic ensures you have a lot of people looking for information about related topics. However, you don't need tons of traffic to make money off your blog. Some blogs make decent enough money with a relatively small audience while others have big audiences and still earn disappointing incomes.

Lastly, profitability. To me, this is the most important factor, because regardless of whatever you achieve with your blog, it is still a business, and needs to make money. You therefore need to blog about a topic around which people are willing to spend money.

From the above, it is clear that while having lots of passion and a ton of traffic around your idea is an added advantage, lack of the same doesn't mean that you can't make money off your blog. The most important thing for your chosen niche is the potential for profitability. People should be willing to spend money in your niche.

So, how do you ensure that your chosen topic will help you make money?

Before I get into how you can go about choosing a profitable niche, I will share something very important that you need to keep in mind. When starting a blog, you should understand that you are not writing for yourself. You are writing for your readers. It is therefore important that you have good knowledge of your target audience, what they like (or despise), and what attracts them to a blog.

Listed here are some of the things that readers want from a blog:

They want to solve a problem. Most people searching for information on the internet have a problem that is bothering them. If you choose to blog about a problem that is common to a number of people and provide a solution that works, you are assured two things: traffic and profitability. There will be a number of people searching for a solution to this problem, and some of them will be willing to pay you if you can take their problem away.

They want to learn something new. Nowadays, when people want to learn something new, they rarely go to a formal class. Instead, they head to the internet to see if they can learn by themselves. If you can effectively teach people something that they are trying to learn, then you already have something to blog about. Is there something you are good at that your peers or colleagues always ask you to help them with? Think of how many other people are faced by the same challenge. You can show them how to go about it on your blog.

They want to reach their goals. Many people have goals they want to reach, but at times they don't know how. Or maybe they know how but lack the motivation to push through. Do you have a goal that you set and achieved? Are there others struggling with the same thing? You can share with them how you achieved your goal and inspire them to push through with theirs.

After choosing an idea that addresses one of these needs, you can then test it for traffic and profitability. How do you do this?

Testing Your Idea For Traffic And Profitability

Find The Search Volume For Your Niche Idea

While it is possible to make money even with a small audience, it is always good to ensure that there is sufficient traffic to keep you going. Therefore, finding the number of people who are searching for things related to your niche idea is a great first step. Since Google is the largest search engine, you should focus on the number of searches done on Google. You can do this using the Google Keyword Planner Tool, which is free tool provided by Google to help people get search data. Simply sign up for an account, click on the "Get search volume data and trends" button and enter your nice idea. You might opt to get data for a specific location or general data for all locations. Once you press the "get search volume" button, you will get data about the number of people searching for your niche idea every month.

This step will give you a general idea of the amount of demand for your niche idea. Keep in mind that this is not keyword research or competitor analysis. You simply want to know to know if people care about your niche idea. The broader your niche idea, the more the search volume you want to see, otherwise you might be in a small niche that doesn't have much money to be spent.

Check Google Trends

Once you know that there is some demand for your niche, the next step is to find out if there is evergreen demand for the niche. To do this, simply go to http://www.google.com/trends and enter your niche idea. This will help you determine if the demand for your niche is rising, falling or stable. Avoid niche ideas with decreasing demand. This step will also help you identify niches that have seasonal demand. You should take the time to understand the reason behind a niche's spike or fall in demand. For instance, some products might have had a spike due to media attention. Such things might mislead you if you don't take time to understand the reason behind these trends. For example, finding out that a niche is not as popular as it once was does not automatically mean that it is no longer profitable. It might simply have gained popularity at a particular time because it went viral, or because it is a seasonal niche.

Find Out If There Are Products On Sale Within The Niche

If a niche is profitable, you will find lots of physical and digital products on sale within the niche. On the other hand, lack of products related to a niche is a sign that there is not money to be made within the niche. You can check for the availability of products related to a niche on sites like Amazon, ShareASale, Ebay, JVZoo, Clickbank, and CJ.com. In this step, you are not looking for a specific volume. Instead, you just want some proof that people spend money in this niche and in what volumes. For instance, you can use Amazon to search for physical products while Clickbank is good for digital products. You can also look for products on Google. Simply Google your niche and check out if the ranking websites are selling any products. If you find that a niche has several products on sale across multiple networks, it is a sign that you are onto a profitable idea. However, you need to go a step further and find out if you can personally make money within the niche. Landing on a profitable niche does not mean that you will automatically make money.

Validate Online Activity Through Popular Websites And Blogs

A niche that has several authority sites and blogs shows that there are a lot of customers in the niche and places to find them. In this step, you want to find sites where potential customers hang out so you can target traffic from these sites. Simply go to the Google search bar and type in your niche idea. Alternatively, you can search for terms like "best {niche idea} blogs" to find the top blogs within the niche. Once you identify the top blogs, find out whether their articles attract a lot of comments and social shares and whether they have a following on social media. What do they sell and how do they make money? This will give you an idea of how interactive the niche is and how easy it will be to connect with customers within the niche.

Find Forums And Message Boards Around The Niche

A niche that has sizable forums and niches around it with active members shows that there is a huge crowd of people who are passionate about the niche and willing to hold discussions around it. Typically, people who are passionate about a topic are always willing to spend money on it. You can find forums and message boards through Google or through sites like FindAForum.net. If you find sizable and active forums, this is a sure sign that there is money to be made in the niche.

Are There Social Media Hubs?

The next step is to find out if there is any activity surrounding your chosen niche on social media sites like Facebook. If there are pages and groups on social media dedicated to a niche, that is a clear sign that the niche has an interactive community who like to connect. These are all potential customers. Once you start your blog, you can share your content to these groups to drive traffic to your blog. Do not restrict yourself to Facebook. Check for your niche on all social media sites, including Instagram, Twitter, Pinterest, Tumblr, Google Plus, Reddit, and so on.

Are People Advertising On Google?

Finally, are there any ads when you search for you niche on Google? A lot of ads is a good sign. People only pay for advertisements if they know they will make their money back. Therefore, if people are paying for Google Ads to advertise their products within that niche, this shows that there is money to be made in the niche.

By running through these steps, you will be able to validate whether your chosen niche is profitable. One thing you should keep in mind is that coming up with a new niche is next to impossible. Therefore, if you find a niche without any products or without other people, it doesn't mean that you have stumbled on an untapped niche. On the contrary, it might mean that there is no money to be made in that niche. A profitable niche will have a significant number of searches, lots of products that sell well, lots of other blogs and websites on the niche, lots of forums and social media activity, as well as people who are paying to advertise products and services related to the niche.

Chapter Summary

- Your blog should be focused on a niche instead of covering a broad topic.
- The key ingredients to choosing a good niche are passion, traffic, and profitability.
- People read blogs because they want to solve a problem, learn something new, or reach their goals.
- You should test your idea for profitability to ensure you don't end up blogging about a topic that has no potential to earn you money.

In the next chapter, you will learn how to choose the perfect name for your blog.

Chapter Three: Choosing The Right Name For Your Blog

In this chapter, you are going to learn how to choose a good name for your blog. This is another problem that most aspiring bloggers face at the very start of their blogging journey.

Coming up with the right name for your blog is very important. It determines the future of your blog and how your visitors will relate with you blog. Unfortunately, for many people, coming up with a good blog name is no easy task. Many are the times you will come up with the perfect name only to conduct a domain search and find out that someone else thought of it long before you. Other bloggers will come up with a name that does not relate to their niche. A good blog name should help potential visitors understand what your blog is about, even without visiting the blog. In this chapter, we are going to look at the process you should follow to come up with a great name for your blog.

It's always advisable to use your blog name as your domain name; therefore, in this guide, there will be an overlap between the blog name and the domain name.

Before we dive in, we need to define something. What makes a good name?

- It should be catchy and memorable.
- It should be short and concise.
- People should be able to read and pronounce it easily.
- People should be able to spell it easily.
- It should help people understand the theme of your blog.
- Opt for a .com domain extension.

Why I Don't Like Blog Name Generators

If you want to avoid the process of coming up with a name for your blog, you can always use a name generator. You simply put in the keywords that describe your blog and it will generate suggestions for you. However, I do not recommend using a blog name generator. I would only advise you to use one if you are looking for a lackluster name for your blog. Blog name generators simply create mash-ups of the words you enter; therefore, they are unlikely to produce any worthwhile names. Unless you are extremely lazy, avoid using blog name generators.

How To Come Up With A Good Blog Name

Now that we know what we are aiming for, let's get down to the process of coming up with the perfect name for your blog. We are going to break down this process into two steps:

- Explore the theme of your blog.
- Vet your chosen name.

Explore The Theme Of Your Blog

Remember, I said that a good blog name should help potential visitors understand the theme of your blog. This first part involves exploring your blog's theme to come up with name ideas.

Write Down A List Of Topics Related To Your Blog

Create a list of the topics you will be blogging about, as well as any other words that are associated to those topics. For instance, if you want to blog about cars, you might come up with words like automobile, tires, engine, motor, driving, speed, petrol, diesel, gear, alloy wheels, drivetrain, sedan, truck, traffic, etc.

The idea is to come up with as many words as you can. Even if you know you are definitely not going to use some of these words, coming up with this list will help spark ideas. Once you are done with the list, cross out the words that you definitely don't want as part of your blog name.

Think Of Your Blog's Tone

Next, take a moment to explore your blog's tone. Your blog's tone is basically how you want your blog to feel and the mood you want it to exude. Tone is defined not by what you say, but by how you say it. It includes your choice of words, how they are arranged, and their rhythm. Blog tones can be casual, serious, funny, sarcastic, you name it.

Once you identify your tone, create another list of words that describe your tone. This will help you come up with a name that matches the feel of your blog.

Think Of Your Target Audience

Next, you need to define your target audience. Who do you want to read your blog? Young dads? Biking enthusiasts? Writers? Think of what your target audience will be seeking on your blog. List the characteristics of your target audience, as well as some of the things they hope to get out of your blog. This step will help you come up with a name that resonates with your readers.

Research The Competition

Look at blogs in the same niche as you and how they are named. The aim of this step is not to steal your competitors' names, but rather to help point your creativity in the right direction. This step will give you a better idea of the kind of names that work and those that do not.

Come Up With A List Of Blog Name Ideas

By now, I'm hoping that you have three lists of words. Go through the lists again and cross out any words that you do not want as part of your blog name. Try coming up with blog name ideas from the remaining words. Now is the time to get creative. Try pairing together two words from different lists. Add a creative prefix or suffix to some words. Play around with the words to create your own new words or add a touch of humor. You can also try using alliteration. For instance, if your blog is aimed at successful young ladies, you could name it "Sweet, Sassy, and Successful." Think outside the box and come up with as many ideas as you can.

Narrow Down Your List

Go through the list of blog name ideas you came up with in the previous step and choose those you think might work. This should be based on your blog's tone, target audience, readability, ease of spelling and pronunciation, as well as memorability.

By the end of this step, you should have three to five appropriate names. Now it's time for step two of our process.

Vet Your Chosen Names

In this step, you will be evaluating your chosen names to make sure they meet all the requirements before making your choice.

The Domain Test

As I mentioned earlier, one of the worst things is coming up with the perfect blog name only to find out that someone else is already using it. Before you proceed, now is the time to check your chosen domains for availability. If two are already taken and the third one is free, your choice has been made for you. If none are available, you will have to go back to the drawing board.

Even if you find that the .com extension of your chosen domain is available, it is important to check the .net and .org extensions of your name to make sure that there aren't other organizations using the same name.

You should also consider how your chosen names look when used as domain names, so you do not end up with an unintentionally inappropriate domain name, such as whorepresents.com (Who Represents) or powergenitalia.com (Powergen Italia). Those are real sites, by the way.

Does The Name Have Staying Power?

Will your chosen name still be relevant a few years down the road? Will it be relevant if you decide to broaden the focus of your blog? Is it bound by a geographical location? For instance, if your blog is aimed at bike riders in Cincinnati and has the name Cincinnati as part of its name, what happens when you want to target riders outside Cincinnati? You should also avoid using trendy words, since that will make your blog seem outdated once the trend shifts to something else.

Does The Name Need A Disclaimer?

When coming up with a name for your blog, think about the long-term growth of your blog. For instance, you could be running a blog for guys who are learning how to play the guitar, but down the road you know that you might start blogging about other instruments as well. In this case, you should avoid using the word guitar in your blog name so you don't have to word the disclaimer: "Well, it's not just for learning the guitar." Ensure that that your blog name doesn't force you to explain that your blog is not what is seems.

Make Your Final Choice

Finally! If a name has made it this far, then you have yourself the right name for your blog. If two or more names made it, then go with the one that feels like the best one for you.

Whether you are searching for a name for your new blog or whether you want to rebrand an existing blog, the process shared in this chapter will help you come up with a good name that you won't regret down the road.

Chapter Summary

- You should use a short, memorable, and simple name that expresses your blog's theme.
- You should opt for a .com extension when choosing your blog name.
- You should explore your blog's theme to give you naming ideas.
- You should vet your chosen blog names before settling on one.

In the next chapter, you will learn how to set up your blog.

Chapter Four: Setting Up Your Blog

In this chapter, you are going to learn how to choose the right blogging platform and how to set up your blog. Now that you have settled on the niche you are going to blog about and have chosen a name for your blog, it is time for you to get down to the actual business of setting up your blog.

Choosing The Best Blogging Platform

The first thing you need to do is to choose the blogging platform that you are going to use for your blog. A blogging platform is a service of software that allows you to publish your content online. It is also a content management system (CMS) that allows you to manage your online content. The kind of blogging platform you opt for depends on how tech savvy you are, as well as the kind of blog you want to build.

Choosing the most appropriate blogging platform is very important. This is because switching from one platform to another can be a headache. If you start on one platform and then later decide that you want to have some features on your blog that are not supported by your current platform, then it will take you a lot of effort and money to move your already-growing blog to another platform. It might also have some implications on your blog's traffic. Therefore, the best thing to do is to ensure that you choose the best platform for you from the very start.

To ensure that you pick the right blogging platform from the beginning of your blogging career, here are some things that you should consider:

Your Goals

The first thing you need to consider before settling on a blogging platform is what you aspire to achieve through your blog. Determining you goals when you are just starting can be a difficult thing to do. However, it will save you a lot of trouble down the road. To help you determine what you want to achieve from your blog, you can ask yourself questions such as:

- Do I intend to blog long-term?
- How do I intend to monetize my blog?
- Is there a chance that I might serve ads on my blog?

Such questions will help you figure out your goals for the blog. You can think of other such questions that take a long-term view at your blogging career. Doing this is very important, because different blogging platforms are better suited for different blogging applications.

Budget

Your choice of blogging platform will also be affected by the amount of money you are willing to spend. When it comes to blogging, there are three main things you might be required to pay for. These are your domain name, hosting for your blog, and the blogging platform you choose to use. However, different blogging platforms have different approaches to this. For instance, some platforms like WordPress.com and Blogger.com are free. This means that you get a domain name, hosting, and access to the platform without having to pay a dime. With others like WordPress.org (this is a different platform from WordPress.com), you get free access to the platform, but then you have to find and pay for your own domain name and hosting. Other platforms like MovableType have a free version as well as a paid version depending on your application of the platform. MovableType also requires you to find your own domain name and hosting.

Apart from paying for the platform, domain name, and hosting, other costs you might incur when setting up your blog include:

Design: All blogging platforms provide free templates that you can apply on your blog. However, if you want a more unique look for your blog, you will need to come up with your own design. If you do not have some web design skills, you will need to hire someone to design the blog for you.

Blog tools: If you want to build a profitable blog, you will need access to some tools to make your work easier and to help you track your blog's progress. While some of these tools are free, you will need to pay for others. At the beginning, you might not really need these tools, but they will definitely come in handy as your blog grows.

Your Technological Know-How

This is another important factor that has a major bearing on your choice of blogging platform. Some blogging platforms are quite technical and complicated, and therefore might be a huge challenge for someone who is trying to build a blog for the first time. Other platforms are a lot simpler and can be used even by beginners, provided you are willing to learn a few basic things.

Of course, even if you are not very technically aligned, you can find someone who is more knowledgeable to lend you a hand. The great thing with blogging is that there is a wide base of communal knowledge around the subject, so you can just join a forum and learn everything you need to know about your chosen platform.

Choosing Between A Hosted And A Standalone Blogging Platform

I mentioned earlier that some blogging platforms will provide you will free hosting (hosted platforms), while others require you to find and pay for your own hosting (standalone platforms). So, what is the difference between the two, and which of them is better?

Hosted Blogging Platforms

Most bloggers start with this kind of platforms, the reason being that such platforms are usually free (or very cheap) and are very easy to use. The most popular hosted blogging platform is Google's Blogger.com. Other examples of hosted blogging platforms include WordPress.com and MSN Spaces.

These platforms are referred to as hosted because they host your blog on their main domain. The URLs for blogs built on hosted platforms usually consist of the blog name and the platform's own URL. For example, if you built a blog named "myblog" on WordPress.com, your blog's URL would be www.myblog.wordpress.com. The wordpress.com extension shows that this blog is hosted on the www.wordpress.com domain instead of standing on its own.

Using a hosted blogging platform has a number of advantages. The first one, obviously, is that most hosted platforms are free. Building a blog on a hosted platform is also relatively easy. They usually come with a basic default template which allows you to set up your blog in a few minutes. Setting up usually involves choosing a template design and filling in a few fields. Anyone can use these platforms, even if you know nothing about the technological side of blogging. They are also very simple to run. They come with very user-friendly features that allow you to create your posts in almost the same way you would do on a word processor. Since they are targeted at beginners, hosted platforms automatically serve their updates. You do not have to upload any new software to the server. Instead, the updates happen seamlessly, sometimes even without your knowledge. Since they are hosted on established domains that already have good page ranks, blogs on hosted platforms are also indexed by such engines pretty quickly.

On the flip side, hosted blogging platforms have a number of disadvantages as well. The first is that they are less customizable than standalone platforms. With a hosted platform, you are stuck with the provided design templates and features. There is not much you can do if you want your blog to have a unique look or extended functionality. This results in many blogs looking very similar to each other. For instance, if you want to make any changes to the default blog templates in Blogger.com, you need to have HTML and CSSS skills.

With hosted platforms, you also have less control over your blog. While the content on your blog is your own, the blog is not technically yours since it is hosted on the platform's domain. This places you at the mercy of the platform, and there is not much you can do. For instance, if the platform's hosting has a problem, your blog might experience some down time, and there's not much you can do about that. The platform also has the right to shut down the blog if they feel that you are in violation of their terms.

I also mentioned that with a hosted platform, your blog URL will include the platform's URL. This robs your blog of much-needed memorability and professionalism. Sure, there are some successful blogs that are built on hosted platforms. However, it comes across as more professional when you have your own custom URL. Finally, upgrading from a hosted to a standalone platform can be much of a challenge. Actually, before you start on a hosted platform, it is good to consider what options you have in case your blog becomes big. Does the hosted platform allow you to easily move to a standalone platform? Remember, changing your domain will also affect some of your traffic, and you will have to start climbing the search engine ranking ladder all over again.

Hosted platforms are best suited for bloggers who do not really care about having their own unique domain and those who are not too concerned with customizing their blogs or adding some unique features. You should also keep in mind that many hosted platforms have strict regulations on how you can monetize your blog. For instance, many do not allow bloggers to serve ads on their blogs. For this reason, I do not recommend using a hosted blogging platform.

Standalone Blogging Platforms

Standalone blogging platforms allow you to host your blog under your own custom domain. The platforms simply provide a CMS for your online content. This is the most preferable option if you intend to build a professional blog. The most popular standalone blogging platform is Wordpress.org.

Using standalone blogging platforms has several advantages. First, it gives you full control over your blog's design. These platforms are very customizable. The only limit to what you can achieve with standalone blogging platforms is your web design skills. If you are not well-versed in web design, you can still use the default templates. Another advantage of standalone platforms is their adaptability. For instance, there is a huge army of developers who are constantly developing all manner of WordPress plugins. The plugins extend the functionality of the basic WordPress installation, allowing you to do achieve and implement all kinds of things on your blog. Many other standalone platforms have their own communities of developers coming up with their own versions of plugins to extend the platforms' functionalities.

Another advantage is that most standalone platforms are free. Sure, you will be required to pay for your own domain name and hosting. However, access to the platform remains free. Finally, you get to have your own custom domain name. This makes your blog URL more memorable, makes your blog come across as more professional, and makes your blog easier to brand.

Despite these advantages, standalone blogging platforms are not without their downsides. First, they can be complicated to set up if you are not very technologically inclined. You will need to purchase your domain name and arrange for your own hosting. Some might require you to set up databases, download the platform to your computer and then upload all the files to your hosting server via FTP

(File Transfer Protocol). However, many have tutorials that can help you with this process. Additionally, many web hosts are now installing these platforms for their users, making the process almost as simple as using a hosted platform.

Another disadvantage of standalone platforms is that you will have to bear the cost of your domain name (a one off registration fee and a yearly renewal fee) as well as the hosting fee (renewed yearly). Luckily, these costs are not very high. When starting, you can get domain name and hosting packages for less than $50 a year However, you might need to switch to a more expensive plan as your blog grows. Updating your platform's version can also be complicated, though most web hosts nowadays have in place systems for automatically installing updates.

Standalone blogging platforms are the best choice for bloggers who want to have their own custom URL and those who want the freedom to customize their blogs as they wish. With a standalone platform, you can configure your blog to look and work very professionally. The only limitation is your imagination and your skills. With standalone platforms, no one has control over your blog, so you can monetize it as you please. I recommend going the standalone route if your intention is to build a professional blog that you will use to earn a living.

With the above knowledge, you should be able to choose the best blogging platform for your needs. In my experience, the best blogging platform is WordPress.org, and I recommend that you use it. It is the most popular blogging platform, powering over 27% of all blogs and websites on the internet. Some reasons behind its popularity are:

- It is free to use (though you have to pay for your domain name and hosting).
- Setting up your blog on WordPress.org is quite easy.
- It has been around for a while and has proven its robustness and security.
- It is supported by a whole industry of developers, designers, and tool providers, helping users achieve more from the platform.

If you choose to build your blog on WordPress, keep in mind that there are two versions of WordPress:

WordPress.com: This is a hosted platform that you can start using without having to pay for anything. Your blog is hosted on the www.wordpress.com domain. You have less control over your blog's design and there are restrictions on the features that you can add and how you monetize your blog.

WordPress.org: This is a standalone platform that gives you control over your blog. Getting a domain name and hosting is up to you. There are no restrictions over how you use or monetize your blog. This is the best option. I am going to use WordPress.org in my explanations.

Getting A Domain Name And Setting Up Your Hosting

Now that you know the blogging platform you are going to use, it is time to pay for your domain name. We already discussed the process of choosing a domain name in the previous chapter, so I won't touch on that. There are several places where you can pay for your domain name. Some good examples include GoDaddy, HostGator, SiteGround, BlueHost, and NameCheap. Visit any of these domain registrars and enter your chosen domain name. If it available, you can go ahead and pay for it.

The next thing is to set up your hosting. It is advisable to have your blog hosted by the same company from which you have purchased your domain name. Once you pay for the hosting, the web host will guide you on how to set up your hosting. Setting up your hosting is a simple process that should not take you more than a few minutes.

Setting Up Your Blog

Once you are done setting up your domain and hosting, the next step is to install WordPress on your blog. Most web hosts have automated the process of installing WordPress, therefore this step should be super easy. You simply need to log into your web host account and find the "Install WordPress" button. Depending on your web host, you might need to select the "do it yourself (FREE)" version. From there, click on the "Install" button. You will be required to enter your domain. After you click on the "Check Domain" button, you will be required to accept the terms and conditions. Click on the checkbox next to the terms and conditions and press the "Install Now" button.

That's all. Once you do that, your blog is up. You can now proclaim to the world that you are a blogger. However, at this point, your blog still looks bland, so you need to make it look much better by installing a theme. WordPress has lots of free themes that you can install on your blog. You can also opt for paid themes if none of the free ones are to your liking.

That's it. Your blog is up and ready. You can now start working on posting your first piece of content.

Chapter Summary

- You should consider your goals, your budget, and your technological know-how when choosing the best blogging platform.
- A standalone blogging platform is preferable if your aim is to build a professional blog.

In the next chapter, you will learn how to create a content

strategy for your blog.

Chapter Five: Creating A Content Strategy For Your Blog

In this chapter, you are going to learn how to create a solid content strategy for your newly created blog.

Let's face it, content is the core of your blog. You cannot be a blogger if you cannot produce content. Unfortunately, creating great content consistently is one of the hardest parts of blogging. One of the major mistakes many beginners make is starting a blog without any plan on how they will create content for it. If you do this, many are the days you will stare at you blog wondering what you should write about. On the other hand, if you have a content strategy, you will have a good idea of what you audience wants to read about and when you need to put up which post.

Having a content strategy is what separates successful bloggers from the rest of the pack. With a content strategy, you won't waste hours creating content that no one cares about or trying to figure out what topic you need to cover next. A study by the Content Marketing Institute reported only 32% of bloggers without a content strategy are effective, compared to 60% of those who have a written content strategy. In this chapter I am going to share seven steps which you can follow to come up with a good content strategy for your blog.

Step 1: Define Your Goals

This is the most important step in creating a content strategy. If you know not where you are going, you will not get there. Without clearly defined goals, the rest of the steps do not really matter. Therefore, take the time to define you blogging goals. What do you want to achieve with your blog? Is your goal to drive customers to your offline business? Is it to create awareness about your services? Is it to generate leads or increase sales? Are you trying to build a brand? Decide on two or three objectives that you want to achieve with your blog. Do not choose more than three objectives. If you do that, your blog will have no central focus, and your chances of achieving success will be greatly diminished.

When defining your goals, be very specific. Simply saying that you want to "generate more leads" for your business is not enough. You need to decide how may leads you want to generate and the timeframe in which you want to do it. In this case, a better goal would be "generate 30% more leads within the next four months". This goal is more specific, is time bound, and is measurable. With such a goal, it becomes easier to determine the kind of content you need to create, the number of people you need to reach, and so on.

Once you have defined your goals, you should then divide them into smaller targets or milestones that you can work towards in the short term. It is easier to follow through when you have small actions that you can take each day. Sometimes, you might need to change your goals.

However, this should be done after you have achieved your current goals.

Step 2: Define Your Ideal Audience

Once you have defined your goals, the next step is to define your ideal target audience. Knowing who you are targeting allows you to create content that appeals to them. Your content will hardly be relevant if you do not know who you are writing for. Knowing who you are writing for also makes it easier for you to promote your content to these people. Many beginners make the mistake of assuming that they know their audience.

Knowing your audience goes beyond knowing that you are writing for motor enthusiasts, bikers, fitness enthusiasts, food lovers, or pet owners. Knowing your readers involves knowing who they are, where thy hang out online, and what their likes and dislikes are. It involves knowing their needs, their desires, their frustrations, their fears, and what they are trying to achieve.

According to Henneke, a business writing coach, you should treat your ideal audience like an imaginary friend.

You should be able to hold a conversation with them the way you do with your close friends. You should be able to tell what gives them joy and what irks them. You should know the questions on their minds before they ask them. Only this way will you be able to connect with them.

When you know your audience's frustrations, challenges, and what they are trying to achieve, it becomes easier to create content that helps them get there. For instance, let's assume that you are a fitness blogger. Different people have different fitness goals. Some could be trying to lose weight, while others could be trying to gain muscle. It is impossible to create content that is relevant to both these two groups. However, if you know that your audience is comprised of the people trying to gain muscle, you can create content that is specifically geared toward helping them do that. This is what it means to know your audience. When starting your blog, you should be very specific about the audience you choose to focus on. Once you smash your goals for this audience, you can then add another similar audience.

Step 3: Come Up With Topic Ideas And Keywords

Now that you know who you are writing for, the next step is to find out what kind of content they like reading and some good keywords you want your content to rank for. When you have some ideas for a number of posts, you will be more organized, and more importantly, you will eliminate the not-so-uncommon sessions of staring at a blank screen wondering what you should write. So, how do you identify keywords and come up with topic ideas?

The first step is keyword research. When most people hear about keyword research, they think it involves entering a phrase they think is relevant and finding other related keywords. This is the wrong approach to keyword research. Your keyword research should be more strategic. Ideally, you want to find the best ranking topics that your readers would be interested in reading. A good way of doing this is to find a competing blog that is both popular and trustworthy. Enter a link to this blog in the Google Keyword Planner tool and you will get a list of their top-ranking keywords, as well as related keywords that are highly searched for and read. Enter these keywords on Google to find the top-ranking articles for these keywords.

Go through these articles to find out what they have in common that makes them successful. In addition, go through the comments and find out what information people are looking for that was missing from these articles.

Another way of finding content that your audience will love is to identify content that is already performing well. You can do this through Buzzsumo. This tool will show you the top performing content for your keywords, as well as the number of shares the content has received. You can also go to Quora and find the most common questions asked by users within your niche or around the keywords you identified. This will give you a general idea of the things that your audience might be interested in learning about. You can also look at some of the best performing posts by your competitors to give you ideas on the hottest topics within your niche.

Step 4: Design Content That Will Get You And Your Audience Closer To Your Goals

Now that you have identified some topics that your audience would love to learn about, it's time to come up with a content plan that will move your audience from where they are (what they are struggling with) to where they want to be (what they want to achieve). The same content will also take you to your goals.

Your content acts as a conveyor belt for your audience by moving them through the following stages:

Awareness – Research – Comparison/Validation – Purchase

Similarly, your content conveyor belt will move your closer to your goals by moving your audience through the following stages:

Stranger – Reader – Subscriber – Loyal Fan – Customer

To effectively move your audience from one phase to another, you need to understand what keeps them stuck in each phase and how your content can help them overcome this obstacle. The content you publish should not merely be treated as content. Instead, you should think of your content as a catalyst that spurs people to achieve specific results. This means that every piece of content you post should have a specific purpose. You will only achieve results with your blogging if you match your content to where your audience members are on their journey.

Look at the blog post ideas you came up with and identify which step of your audience's journey they match. Organize these topics in such a way that they will help move your audience through the various stages.

Step 5: Determine The Best Format For Your Content

When people think of blogging, they automatically think of serving their content as written posts. However, have you considered whether your audience might have greater preference for other content formats? Apart from text, you can also serve your content as audio, video, or even as presentations.

Apart from the actual medium of content presentation, there are other considerations that you also need to keep in mind. Does your ideal audience prefer short posts or longer, more detailed ones? Have you thought of incorporating images in your posts? Have you thought of incorporating listicles and case studies as part of your content? All these have an impact on the ability of your content to reach your ideal audience.

So, how do you decide which format is best for you blog? Again, you can glean this information from your competitors. Look at your competitors' blogs and try to find out the content formats that their audiences are most receptive to. Go through the comments on their blog posts and look for clues as to the kind of content their followers are most interested in. Once you have built a significant readership, you can also post a survey to your readers asking them what their preferences are. You can also visit forums within your niche to find out the kind of content the members are sharing. All these strategies will help you come up with the correct content profile to help you grow your blog.

Step 6: Create An Editorial Calendar

Another major mistake most beginners make is to post randomly on their blogs. The problem with this is that you tend to lose focus and prioritize other things over your blog. To prevent this, you need to create an editorial calendar. This is a posting schedule detailing when you will post and which post needs to be posted on which day. An editorial calendar helps you keep yourself on track and ensures that all your posts are published on time.

Since you have already come up with a list of (hopefully 15 to 20) blog post ideas and decided the order in which you are going to post them, all that is left is to decide when each post will be published. When coming up with an editorial calendar, you should consider your lifestyle. Don't come up with a schedule that you know will be difficult for you to follow. Instead, go for one that allows you to remain consistent. For instance, posting an article every day might sound awesome, but can you really manage that? Will you even have enough time to promote each post?

I would recommend working with a posting schedule of two to four posts every month. This gives you enough time to come up with high-quality posts, as well as to promote your posts every time you publish. With a schedule of two posts per month, the 15 to 20 post ideas you came up with will take you through seven to 10 months, which is enough time to build a decent amount of traffic. Whatever posting schedule you settle on, make sure that it is workable for you, and ensure that you stick to it.

There are several tools that you can use for your editorial calendar. A good editorial calendar should be able to give you a bird's eye view of your posting schedule. It shows you all the planned posts, when each post is due and the stage of the audience journey that it is targeted for. If there are people helping you to create content, your editorial calendar should also be able to give you visibility into who is working on which piece of content. Some free tools you can use to create your editorial calendar include Google Calendar or Trello. If you are looking for a more dedicated calendar with an extended set of features, you can check out CoSchedule.

Step 7: Create Amazing Content

You have defined your goals, you thoroughly know and understand your ideal audience, you have done your keyword research, you have your topics, and you have created your content calendar. Now is time to go ahead and create amazing content for your audience.

There are a number of things that separate great content from ordinary, run-of-the-mill content. Great content is well written, with correct spelling and grammar and with simple language that is easy to understand. It is well researched and makes use of examples, case studies, and useful stats. It utilizes media to help your audience grasp the concepts better. Finally, great content is properly formatted for easy readability.

It might be tempting to create and publish content randomly as it comes to mind. However, having a clear content strategy will save you hours of time and lots of headache. You will also be more effective when you follow a content strategy. You will be better prepared and your blogging career will be a lot more fun when you know what you are supposed to be doing instead of stumbling in the dark. The best part is that coming up with a good content strategy only takes a few hours.

Chapter Summary

- Your blogging will be more effective when you have and stick to a content strategy.
- The first step of being a successful blogger is to define what you want to achieve from your blog.
- You can only create the right content when you know the exact audience you are creating the content for.
- You should take the time to find relevant keywords and come up with a number of blog post ideas before you publish your first post.
- You should design content that will help transform your audience.
- It is always good to take time to understand the content format that is most relevant to your audience.

- You should have an editorial calendar to keep you on track.

In the next chapter, you will learn how to drive traffic to your blog.

Chapter Six: Building Traffic

In this chapter, you are going to learn how to attract traffic and build an audience for your blog.

Making money from blogging involves two things: building an audience and then selling them something. Now that you have set up your blog and written a few pieces of content, it is time to find readers. The mistake most new bloggers make is that they create great content, share it with their friends on their social media pages, and wait for a ton of traffic to flood to their blog. Sadly, this never happens, and many of them give up as a result. You need to understand that creating great content is only half the battle. You also need to aggressively promote your content.

As the popular saying in blogging circles goes, content might be king, but promotion is queen.

So, how do you get people to start reading your blog posts? Below are some tried and tested techniques that are guaranteed to grow your blog's traffic over time.

Offer Valuable Content

In the previous chapter, I mentioned that you should make sure you create great content. I will reiterate this because it is crucial to building an audience for your blog. You should make sure that the posts on your blog provide your readers with meaningful and useful information that is relevant to their lives. Remember, people are on your blog because they want to learn something new, solve a problem, or achieve their goals. Your blog posts should help them do that.

Unfortunately, most new bloggers do not do this. They take the same content that is on a hundred other blogs and rehash it. If your content is the same as the content on a hundred other blogs, why should I bother reading it? Find a way to create content that is unique to your blog. Avoid plagiarizing content from other bloggers. Instead, take trending topics within your industry and dissect them in your own personal voice. Experiment with different types of content formats and find out what works best.

Consistency

The second most important thing you should keep in mind is keeping your blog regularly and consistently updated. The posting frequency is not really a huge concern. You can decide on a posting schedule that works best for you, whether that is daily, weekly, or monthly. Once you decide on a certain posting schedule, make sure you follow it religiously. If you post inconsistently or decrease your posting frequency for some reason, your traffic is going to take a hit. The worst part about this is that to overturn the decline in traffic resulting from one month of inconsistency, you will need several months of consistent posting.

SEO

Search engines are a major source of traffic; therefore, it is important for you to make sure that potential readers can find your blog and your posts on search engines. Every single day, people perform over seven billion searches on Google. By optimizing your blog and posts for search engines, you can direct some portion of this massive traffic to your blog. SEO is a complex and multi-faceted element. However, there are some easy SEO strategies that will go a long way in driving traffic to your blog. One of these is doing proper keyword research and ensuring that you include these keywords in your blog post content, title, and Meta descriptions. If your post contains images, include the keywords as part of the image name instead of using generic names like "kdhfk.jpg". You should also include relevant tags in your posts. There are some free WordPress plugins you can use to automate your blog's SEO, such as the Yoast Wordpress SEO plugin.

Blog Commenting

Blog commenting involves reading posts and leaving comments on the posts, with a link back to your blog. Blog commenting does two things. First, it is a great way of establishing relationships with other bloggers in your niche. Second, leaving relevant comments on posts by high-authority bloggers can send lots of traffic to your blog. To implement this technique, come up with a list of the most relevant blogs in your niche. Regularly read the posts on these blogs, leave comments, and interact with other people commenting on these blogs. Do not leave one-line comments that do not add value to the posts. Instead, write detailed comments that add information to the post or that answer questions posed by other commenters. If you do it regularly, the other bloggers and their visitors will soon notice your expertise in your field and some of them will definitely visit your blog. Depending on the kind of comments you leave, you might even get a chance to guest post on these top blogs, something that can drive huge traffic to your blog.

Article Marketing

This is another easy technique that can drive lots of traffic to your blog if it is done properly. This technique involves creating short articles within your niche and distributing them to free article marketplaces. These articles are a great way to showcase your expertise in your industry. These articles are usually accompanied by an author by-line that consists of your bio and a link back to your blog, giving you the chance to tell people about yourself and to direct them to your blog. Since these articles will be distributed all over the internet, they help you to reach audiences that you would have been unable to reach through other means.

Guest Blogging

This is one of the best and the most effective ways of growing traffic to your blog. Guest blogging essentially involves tapping into the traffic of established bloggers in your niche who have more traffic than you. Guest blogging helps you showcase your expertise, lets people interested in your niche know about your blog, and drives some of these people to your blog. The backlinks generated from guest posting also contribute to your SEO. To implement this technique, make a list of successful blogs with a huge and engaged audience within your niche. Reach out to the owners of these blogs and pitch your guest post ideas. Make sure to show them how they will benefit from your guest post. Once they agree to your pitch, go ahead and create a unique and high-quality post. Once the post is up on their blog, promote it the same way you promote posts on your own blog. Make sure to engage with readers who comment on the post and respond to their questions.

Invite Other Bloggers To Guest Post On Your Blog

This is the inverse of the previous technique. Instead of reaching out to top bloggers within your niche with the aim of writing guest posts on their blogs, pitch to them the idea of them writing a guest post on your blog. Once the post is live, there is a high likelihood that they will promote it to their audience, bringing loads of traffic to your blog. If you have more amazing content on your blog, some of their audience might also end up becoming loyal fans of your blog.

Social Media

Today, almost every person with access to the internet is active on one social media platform or another. You can take advantage of all these users to drive traffic to your blog. Create social media profiles for your blog on the platforms where your target audience are most likely to be found. These include sites like Facebook, Instagram, Twitter, Pinterest, Google+, Tumblr, and LinkedIn. With its over 2.2 billion active users, Facebook is my favorite. However, do not restrict yourself to Facebook. Every time you put up a new post, share it on your social media profiles. Once you create a habit of regularly sharing great content on your social media profiles, this can easily become your biggest source of traffic.

Here are some strategies you can use to get more results from social media:

Share your content severally: Once you put up a post on your blog, share it on all the platforms on which you are active. Customize each update for its specific platform. For instance, you can include hashtags when posting on Instagram and Twitter, though this wouldn't work on Facebook. You should also share these updates a couple of times on each platform, with a few days or weeks between each update.

Ride on new social features: When social media platforms launch new features, these features attract a lot of attention. Good examples of these are Twitter moments and Instagram stories. You can ride on the popularity of these new features to drive more traffic to your blog.

Each update should be unique: While I said that you should share each post a couple of times on social media, the updates should not be identical. Change the caption every time you share it to appeal to a wider audience.

Forums

Another great source of traffic is online forums. Forums are places where people interested in a topic meet to discuss matters related to the topic. The top forums in most niches usually have hundreds of thousands of members. They are also visited by millions of people each month. You can take advantage of forums to drive some of this traffic to your blog. However, to do this, you need to have the right approach. Do not simply start posting links to your blog in every post on the forum. This is seen as being spammy and might even get you kicked out of the forum. Instead, after joining the forum, take some time to learn how it operates. Interact with other members by contributing to discussions and answering the questions posed by other members. Do this for a while before you start sharing links to your blog. Once you start sharing links, use your forum signature. Since the members have already seen you and your contributions on the forum, many of them are going to click through to your blog.

Influencer Marketing

Sometimes, you will come across blogs that seem to come out of nowhere, and in a very short time, they are among the top blogs in that niche and are considered as thought leaders in their industries. How do they achieve this in such a short time? In most cases, the bloggers behind them take advantage of the power of influencer marketing. Rather than following the slow and steady route of building an audience by consistently sharing their content on social media for a long time, they take a short cut by connecting with industry movers and shakers. Influencer marketing involves reaching out to reputable figures within your industry and having them share your content. Since these figures are already known and trusted within your niche, sharing your content is seen as an endorsement for your blog. Their huge following will flock to your blog. This is one of the quickest ways of growing your audience and building your blog's authority.

Content Repurposing

Most bloggers confine themselves to written content. The problem with this is that by doing so, you confine yourself to a small portion of your potential audience. Some people might not be huge fans of reading online content, but maybe they enjoy watching video content. By converting your content into multiple formats, you are able to reach a wider audience. For example, after creating a blog post, you can record a video of yourself discussing the information shared in the blog post and share the video on YouTube. You can then share an audio version of the video as a podcast. You can compress the information from your blog post into a slide deck and post it on SlideShare. You can design the slide deck into a magazine and post it on FlipBoard. If you do all this, you will reach five different audiences from five different platforms, whereas you would have only reached a single audience of you stopped at creating a blog post.

One thing you should keep in mind is that you should post on these other platforms in addition to your blog. You should also link back to your blog from these other platforms. This way, you have a chance of converting your inbound links to customers. If you do not link to your blog, someone will watch your video on YouTube and then move on to other videos. That is a lost opportunity.

Optimize Your Content For Clicks And Shares

To increase the traffic on your blog, you also need to ensure that your content is optimized to get more social media shares and repeat visits. How do you do this? First, you should ensure that most of your posts are based on evergreen content. Evergreen content is content that is relevant all year round, and even a couple of years down the line. Sure, you can get lots of initial traffic from seasonal posts, trending topics, and breaking news. However, evergreen content drives more traffic in the long run. Since it will be relevant even a year after you post it, it is also likely to receive shares for much longer.

Another technique to optimize your content for more clicks is to serialize your blog posts. This means that you should create a series of continuous posts. By dangling subsequent parts of your series in front of your readers, you can increase your email subscriptions. Serialized posts are usually comprehensive and very valuable. Therefore, even if you do not use them to drive email subscriptions, your visitors are likely to share these posts and check back on them severally as they try to solve their problem.

Email List Building

This is one of the most reliable sources of traffic for bloggers. It is also one of the most effective tools for converting visitors into customers. Sadly, this is something that is often ignored by newbie bloggers. If you want to get ahead of the pack, you should start building your email list immediately after launching your new blog. Why is email so effective? With the increasing dependence on mobile devices, more and more people are reading their emails on mobile. Therefore, through email, you can reach your audience at any time of the day, regardless of where they are. Every time you put up a new post on your blog, share it with your subscribers via email. People who have taken the liberty to subscribe to your email list have already demonstrated that they are interested in your content. Therefore, they are more likely to click through to your post. They are also more likely to comment on your posts and share them with their followers on social media. Research has shown that email subscribers share content 3.9 times more than other visitors.

Partnerships

You can also drive free traffic to your blog by getting into partnerships with other bloggers within your niche. There are several blog networks out there. All you need to do is to identify and become a member of the most relevant ones in your niche. Apart from joining blog networks, you should reach out to other bloggers within your niche and get into partnerships where each of you promotes the other's posts to your audience. This means that you should continuously try to connect with other top bloggers in your niche. Some of them won't accept your request, and that is fine. However, if you have something to bring to the table, many will accept, and both of you will be able to increase traffic to your blogs.

Run Contests

When you have just launched a new blog, it is very important to create some buzz around it. There is no better way of doing this than giving people an incentive for visiting your blog. This is where contests come in. Contests require visitors to engage with your blog in some way (commenting, sharing your posts, or subscribing to your emails) in order to be eligible to receive some prizes. Find something that you can give out and promote your contest on social media. People love free things, and they are definitely going to check out and engage with your blog if that means the possibility of winning a prize.

Budget For Ads

The methods mentioned so far are free methods of driving traffic to your blog. However, if you want to see faster results and if you have the money to spend, you should put up paid ads on your blog's social media channels. Most social media platforms have a way of determining what their users see on their timelines. However, through targeted ads, you can reach a more targeted audience that is relevant to your niche. Facebook is a particularly great platform for paid ads since it has excellent targeting and a wide reach. You do not have to pay for ads every single day. However, with a relatively small budget, you can drive lots of traffic to your blog through paid ads.

Watch Your Analytics

It is of no use to drive traffic to your blog if you do not keep track of your traffic statistics. You can keep track of your blog's traffic statistics through your site's built-in statistics or through free apps like Google Analytics. Find out the most popular posts and identify the common factor between them. Try to replicate this in your other posts. Analytics will also show you where most of your traffic is coming from. You can then focus your efforts on those platforms. If you find that some other blogs are driving traffic to your blog, reach out to them and thank them for promoting your content. You can also point them to some other relevant posts that they might have overlooked. Without tracking your traffic and engagement metrics, it will be very difficult to determine what works and what you need to improve.

Chapter Summary

- It is important to offer valuable content with your blog.

- It is important to maintain consistency in your posting.
- You should use proper SEO to drive traffic from search engines.
- You can direct traffic from other blogs to your blog through blog commenting.
- You can drive extra traffic to your blog through article marketing.
- You should borrow traffic from established blogs through guest blogging.
- You should leverage social media to boost your traffic.
- Dropping links in forums is a great way of driving traffic to your blog.
- You can take a short cut to grow your traffic through influencer marketing.
- Content repurposing can help you reach a wider audience.
- Your content should be optimized for clicks and shares.
- Your email list is the most reliable source of traffic. Build it.

- You should get into partnerships with other bloggers.
- Contests are a great way of building buzz around your blog.
- If you have the money to spend, you should use paid ads for quicker results.
- You should always track your traffic and engagement metrics.

In the next chapter, you will learn various ways through which you can monetize your blog.

Chapter Seven: Turn Your Audience Into Revenue

In this chapter, you are going to learn how to turn your blog's audience into money. This section is very important. It does not matter how many people you are able to attract to your blog. If you cannot turn them into a source of income, then you are not in business.

In the previous chapter, I mentioned that making money from your blog involves building an audience and then selling them something. This basically means that your blog is a lead generation machine. Now that you have already built an audience for your blog, how do you make money from them? Below are a number of ways through which you can monetize your blog.

Selling Advertisements

This is most common model for monetizing a blog. If you ask most bloggers who earn an income from their blog, they will tell you that advertising was the first thing they tried once they were ready to monetize their blogs. Advertising on your blog is similar to placing advertisements on a newspaper or magazine. You simply need to place little advertisement banners on your blog. Every time one of your visitors clicks on these ads, you earn a few cents or dollars.

One common thing among all advertisers is that they love numbers. Therefore, if your blog attracts significant amounts of traffic, advertisers will have no problem paying you in exchange for putting their products or services in front of all the eyeballs that land on your blog. If you have lots of traffic, you can negotiate a direct deal with advertisers. If your traffic is not enough to warrant a direct deal with advertisers, you can still make some serve ads on you blog by joining ad networks. A good and very popular example is Google AdSense. Apart from placing banner ads on your blog, you can also serve advertisements as inline text ads, which are placed naturally within your content.

Despite being the most common and most popular means of monetizing your blog, selling advertisements is not very effective. I actually do not recommend it. With PPC (pay per click) ads, you only earn a few cents for every click. Keep in mind that only a small portion of your visitors will click on these ads. Therefore, unless you have traffic running into the millions of visitors per month, you are unlikely to make any significant amount of money. Additionally, most people hate banner ads. Many have installed ad blocking programs on their computers, which means they won't see or click on your ads, which translates to even less revenue for you.

Another reason why you should avoid advertisements is that they do not add any value to your readers. On the contrary, they try to divert your readers' attention from the information on the post. In addition, by serving PPC ads on your blog, you are actually diluting your efforts. Imagine spending months to build a significant amount of traffic to your blog, and then sending them away to another site in exchange for a few cents. Selling ads on your blog is akin to setting up a nice storefront in town, then telling the customers who walk in to visit another store down the street. Doesn't make a lot of sense.

This does not mean that there is no money to be made through selling advertisements. There are people who certainly make good money from it. However, unless you are in a niche that has few other options, I do not recommend this model of monetization. Some niches that only lend themselves to advertising include celebrity and politics-related niches.

Affiliate Marketing

This is another model of monetization that has become very popular in recent times. Affiliate marketing essentially involves recommending other people's products to your audience. You get your own personal affiliate link which you place on your blog. This personal link makes it possible for the product owner to track the people that you refer to their product. If one of your referrals clicks on your affiliate link and makes a purchase, you get a commission on that sale.

Affiliate marketing has grown in popularity because:

- You do not have to concern yourself with creating a product.
- Fulfillment and support issues will be handled by the seller.
- You can choose the best products and avoid mediocre products.

If you decide to monetize your blog through affiliate marketing, there are a couple of things you should keep in mind. If you want to be a successful affiliate marketer, you should promote the products the same way you would promote your own products. Do not promote a product simply because you want to earn a commission. Only promote a product if it is relevant to your niche and only if you are certain that it will actually be helpful to your readers.

If affiliate marketing is your preferred business model, you blog should be focused on helping your readers move from an unwanted "before" state to a desired "after" state. This does not matter what niche you are in. Every niche has problems that people want to overcome. You should then find the challenges that people face trying to get from the before state to the after state and recommend products that help them to overcome these challenges. You should create content that helps these people get to their desired state with the help of the products you are promoting.

There are several affiliate networks that you can join and find products to promote. Some of the most popular are Amazon Associates, Commission Junction, ShareASale, and ClickBank. Find an affiliate network that works for you, become a member, find appropriate products to promote, and start making money from your blog. Before joining, take the time to review the terms of each affiliate network to find one that is most favorable to you.

Offer Coaching Services

If you want to start earning from your blog in the shortest time possible, this is one of the best monetization methods. Coaching involves offering clients personal access to your expertise to help them solve a problem or achieve their goals. With coaching, you don't need thousands of visitors to start earning from your blog. All you need is to convince a handful of people about your expertise and you will be on your way to earning a significant income. Coaching is very lucrative, with data from Disc Insights showing that the personal coaching industry brings in about $2 billion in revenue every year.

Regardless of whatever niche you are in, people will experience one challenge or the other. People want to improve different aspects of their lives or learn new skills. By offering to walk with them and give them your personal help to ensure they achieve their objectives, you can make yourself good money. For instance, a freelance writer might need a business coach to teach him the best ways of marketing his services, how to charge the best rates, and how to retain existing clients. The good thing with coaching is that the results of coaching are noticeable, which is why there is such a high demand for coaching services. Moreover, if you help people achieve their goals, they are very likely to send a lot of referrals your way, thereby increasing your customer base without any extra effort on your part.

So, how do you turn your blog into a coaching business? First, you should focus on creating relevant and useful content on matters affecting the clients and prospects you are targeting. For instance, if your coaching business is targeted to freelance web developers, you can cover topics like how to attract new clients, how to market their freelance services online, how to generate and capture leads, how to brand themselves, how to get rid of difficult clients, and so on.

Second, you should have a strong value proposition. Coaching is already a saturated industry. Therefore, you need something to set yourself apart from other coaches, a good reason why your clients should work with you instead of others. To do this, you need to prove your expertise by consistently sharing great content that takes people closer to their objectives. If people can learn and get closer to their objectives by simply reading your posts, then there is much more they can learn by getting coached by you.

Sell Online Courses

This is another way of making good money from your blog even if you don't have a ton of traffic. You can start making money with as little as 50 visitors per day. To get started, you should find out the most pressing challenges faced by your readers and then create a course that helps them solve these problems. The problem with most bloggers is that they obsess so much about producing the perfect course that they end up coming up with nothing. Understand that your first course probably won't be that good, and that's alright. Just get started. You will improve as you get used to creating and selling courses.

You might have worries that the information you want to sell in your course is available elsewhere for free. That doesn't matter. People like convenience and have no problem paying for it. If you can collect all the information required to achieve something, organize it, and package it nicely, complete with action steps on how to apply the information, there will be people willing to pay for it. In addition, people perceive online courses as having more value than blog posts. If you took the time to create an online course, then certainly it must offer more value than a blog post that was hastily put together. Therefore, you should not be afraid of creating an online course, even if you feel that your topic has been covered by others.

You should not worry about your experience either. The very fact that you run a blog that helps people overcome a particular challenge or achieve their goals is enough proof that you know what you are talking about. Therefore, you should go the next step and upgrade your blogging career by offering online courses.

If you decide to go the online course route, you should be aware that the online course market is constantly evolving. You should know that there are some popular platforms for selling online courses – such as Teachable, Udemy, and Course Merchant – and find out how they will affect your business model. You can choose to sell your online course on these platforms and use your blog to promote your course or you can opt to sell it directly through your blog. However, you should keep in mind that these platforms have a much wider audience that you might be able to reach with your blog, especially if it is a relatively new blog. Some premium online course plugins that you can use to host your course on your WordPress blog are Woothemes Sensei, WP CourseWare, Coursepress, Zippy Courses, and so on. To be successful with online courses, you should make sure that your courses are unique, useful, and engaging.

Become An In-Demand Freelance Blogger

You already have your own blog and you have managed to build a significant audience for it. This means that you already have the necessary skills to become a highly sought-after freelance blogger. Many brands know that blogging is an effective way of boosting their online sales, yet they lack personnel with the relevant skillset to blog for them. These brands would be willing to pay you a fortune to become their freelance blogger. Being a freelance blogger is different from being a freelance writer. A freelance writer is tasked with creating content for blog posts, landing pages, email marketing campaigns, and so on. A freelance blogger, on the other hand, is involved with everything that concerns a brand's blog, from coming up with a content strategy, creating the content and promoting it, to engaging with the blog's audience and building a community of loyal followers. A freelance blogger delivers more value, and you can bet they are compensated accordingly.

Businesses are beginning to understand the importance of content marketing. According to data from B2C, 54% of B2B marketers are set to increase their content marketing budget over the next year. Estimates show that marketers already spend about $44 billion on content marketing. This shows that the demand for content will only keep increasing. Therefore, you can make a killing by positioning yourself as a freelance blogger, something that is still largely unexplored territory.

You might be thinking that this field is saturated owing to the high number of freelance writers on the internet. However, being a freelance blogger requires more than simply being a good writer. You need to be conversant with WordPress, social media, SEO, and so on. You also need to be persuasive. If you have these skills, you have everything you need to be a highly sought-after freelance blogger.

To get started, you will need to aggressively market your services. You can do this through social media marketing, consistent posting on your blog, guest blogging on reputable blogs, and even using paid ads. However, once you start getting clients, you financial well-being will take a turn for the better.

Create A Members' Area

This is a good way of ensuring that you have a long term and dependable income from your blog. Creating a members' area on your blog turns it from simply being a lead generation machine into an actual virtual storefront. Before you create a members' area on your blog, you need to come up with a high-value feature, such as one-on-one coaching or premium content. You can then go ahead and create a members' area that gives readers who pay a monthly fee access to this high-value feature.

Doing this has a number of benefits. First, it takes much less time, money and effort to maintain the members' area than to look for new sales each and every month. You will also get a higher lifetime value from your clients. This is because you will continue earning from a client for months or years after acquiring them, as opposed to the single revenue gained from a one-time client at the time of purchase. Finally, a members' area gives you a recurrent revenue stream, allowing you to have a more predictable income from your blog.

Create And Sell Kindle Books

A lot of people are making money with Amazon Kindle publishing, and you can do so, too, with the help of your blog. The revenue from eBook sales has been on an upward trend, and you can expect that it will continue rising. With 47% of eBooks being read on Amazon Kindle, there's a lot of money to be made through Kindle publishing. The good thing with selling eBooks on Kindle is that there is a ready market of buyers stretching into the millions. Since Amazon is already a trusted shopping site, you do not have to expend a lot of effort convincing people of your credibility. By selling your eBooks on Amazon Kindle, Amazon's credibility is passed on to your book.

So, how does Amazon Kindle tie to your blog? You can make more sales on Amazon Kindle by using your blog to market your eBooks. You can give discounts to your readers as well as free copies of your eBook. This is especially important when you want to generate reviews for your book. Since your readers have already engaged with you, they are more likely to leave reviews on your books, something that is critical if you are to make good sales. You can also use your blog to build some buzz for your book before your launch it. With your blog's audience, influence, and authority, you can short cut your way to earning a good income selling eBooks on Amazon Kindle.

If you choose to go the Kindle way, you should be prepared to put in lots of hard work. This is because you will need to publish high-quality books regularly. The more books you have on sale, the more you are likely to earn. Kindle books are priced pretty cheaply, so you need to make a lot of sales to generate significant revenue. However, it is still very much possible to earn good money from Kindle eBooks. You can even earn without having to write a single book. All you need to do is to hire a ghost writer to create the books for you and then focus on using your blog to drive sales for your books.

Paid Posts

Another way of generating some income from your blog is to put up paid reviews or paid posts. This is something that is very common in niches where there is a huge focus on community and a lot of reading, and where people buy a lot of stuff. A good example is the "mommy blog" niche.

Blogging is a very powerful branding tool. In some niches (like the mommy blog niche), there are several top bloggers who have created huge brands without selling any products. These bloggers usually wield a lot of influence over their readers. Therefore, for companies who want to promote their products, it makes a lot of sense to reach out to these top bloggers and pay them to talk about their products.

If you are in such a niche, you can opt to go this route. If you put up a paid post, it is good to fully disclose to your readers that you are getting financial compensation for the post. Otherwise, it can lead to loss of trust from your audience, which is something that you want to avoid. My advice is, if you are going to put up paid posts, the best thing to do is to market your service as a package. Consider your various exposure tools such as your blog, your email list and your social media channels. Create various packages that give the advertiser different levels of exposure. This way, you are able to charge higher fees for your services.

Speaking Gigs

Once you have established your expertise and authority in a specific niche through your blog, you can use this authority to get paid for speaking gigs. In this case, the purpose of your blog is to build your credibility as an expert in your niche. However, you need to keep in mind that your target customers in this case are not your readers, but rather event organizers.

However, this model is not perfect for all bloggers since not everyone is a great speaker. Some bloggers are not even comfortable speaking in front of people. However, it is still a lucrative model for monetizing your blog.

If you decide to follow this route, you should not forget that you real customers are event organizers who want great speakers for their event and ticket sales resulting from your influence and reputation. The best and highest-paid speakers are those who can fill all the seats. Therefore, you should spend lots of effort branding yourself through your blog. You should also include a page on your blog selling your services as a speaker. Include videos of yourself speaking at previous events, as well as testimonials from those events. In this case, you are the product, and you therefore sell yourself.

Events

This is related to the previous strategy in some way. Though it has yet to become very popular, a number of bloggers have started turning to events to increase their revenue. Once you have built your credibility and established your expertise through your blog, you can then go ahead and hold an event such as a live workshop, a webinar, an online summit, a conference, or a seminar. You then sell tickets to the event or charge the attendees some fees in the case of online events. If the content on your blog is helpful, relevant ad interesting, people will be willing to pay in order to learn something from you. They key here is to have established your expertise on your niche.

Apart from charging attendees, you can also earn some money by finding individuals or organizations to sponsor your event. You can also earn some extra money by promoting your other products during these events. In addition, you can invite guest speakers to your events and earn commissions from the sales made as a result of marketing their products at your event.

Selling Services

I have mentioned severally that blogging is a perfect way of showcasing your expertise in a given industry. Therefore, if you have a service that you can provide, you can build credibility for your services and attract potential customers through your blog. For instance, if you provide SEO consultancy services, your blog should be focused on sharing informational and helpful content on how to optimize websites for search engines. Your blog should act as a resource for site admins, web masters and bloggers. In this case, if a blogger needs someone to improve their blog's SEO, who do you think they will turn to? You, of course, because they know that you are an expert when it comes to SEO.

This model is perfect for any blogger who has a service they can provide. It is particularly great for freelancers, such as web developers, copywriters, graphic designers, and so on.

Promoting An Offline Business

Remember, the main purpose of a blog is to generate leads. Once you generate leads, you can then go ahead and sell them something. You do not have to restrict yourself to selling products from an online business. You can also sell products from an offline business. In this case, you are simply using your blog to help your offline business reach an online audience. If you think of it, you will notice that many physical businesses have websites. Similarly, there are many brick-and-mortar businesses that promote their products and services on social media. Therefore, the idea of promoting your brick-and-mortar business through your blog is not so alien. Reports show that before making an offline purchase, about 64% of shoppers research the products online. You can use your blog to direct these shoppers to your offline business. Promoting your offline business through your blog is also a good way of building your brand, cultivating trust with your customers, and boosting your business's authority.

Blog Flipping

Finally, you can build your blog from scratch, build some significant traffic around it, and then sell it. Actually, there are some people who specialize in buying dead or underutilized blogs. These people then go to work, creating content for these blogs, optimizing them for search engines and generally promoting them. Once these blogs start attracting significant amounts of traffic, they sell them for a profit. This is what is known as blog flipping.

If you decide to try your hand at blog flipping, then I recommend that you focus on blogs that have some traffic but have been neglected by their owners. Such people usually feel a little guilty for neglecting their blogs. In most cases, they are also not aware that they can make some money by selling their blogs. You can approach such people with an offer to buy their blogs. Let them know that you are willing to run the blog and continue providing value to their readers. To such people, this is usually seen as a win-win situation. They will almost always agree to your offer. Once you acquire it, do your magic, turn it around into an effective marketing platform, and then sell it for a handsome profit.

However, if you try to create a new blog from scratch, populate it with a few pieces of content and try to sell it as a blog that has "huge potential," you are unlikely to make any significant income. Only a newbie can buy such a site that has no significant traffic.

Other Income Streams

In this chapter, I have shared the most common models that you can use to monetize your blog. The list is not comprehensive. Blogging is a dynamic industry, and new ways of monetizing will keep coming up every day. For instance, some bloggers make money by asking for donations from visitors. Others earn their revenue by syndicating content to other sites. There is no shortage of ways through which you can earn from your blog.

Finally, you should keep in mind that if you want to make it as full-time blogger, you should not depend on one source of income. Implement different models to diversify your revenue streams. Try several models and find out what works best for you. For instance, you might put up online courses for sale, sell your services, have a member's area, and engage in some affiliate marketing. This helps you spread your risk and makes your journey to full dependence on your blog much quicker. With multiple income streams, you can easily start bringing in over $100,000 from your blog.

Chapter Summary

- Selling advertisements is not a very effective method of monetizing your blog.
- You can easily make money from your blog through affiliate marketing.
- Offering coaching services is one of the best methods if you want to start earning money from your blog in the shortest time possible.
- Selling online courses is another way of making good money from your blog even if you don't have a ton of traffic.
- By building your own blog from scratch to a significant readership, you already have the

necessary skills to start making money as a highly sought-after freelance blogger.

- Creating a member's area on your blog is a good way of ensuring that you have a long-term and dependable income from your blog.
- You can create Kindle eBooks and use your blog to promote them and drive sales.
- You can also make money from your blog by putting up paid posts.
- If you are a great speaker, you can make money by getting paid for speaking gigs.

Chapter Eight: Eight Common Mistakes To Avoid

In this chapter, you will learn about some common mistakes that most beginner bloggers make and how to avoid them.

To many people, blogging looks like an easy thing to do, until they actually start doing it. Once you get started, you will come across multiple hurdles and unexpected roadblocks that you have to overcome. You will also make a couple of mistakes. To build a profitable blog, you will have to be on a constant learning curve, therefore mistakes are inevitable. Actually, some of your greatest learning experiences will come from your mistakes. However, this is not to say that you should plough ahead making mistakes even when you can avoid them. Instead of making the same mistakes that everyone makes, why not learn from the experiences of others and save yourself some money and time?

Listed here are some of the mistakes that are common to newbie bloggers, along with some pointers on how you can avoid them.

Mistake 1: Failing To Define Your Target Audience

Most bloggers have absolutely no idea who their target audience is, which in turn means that they cannot produce the right content. How do you create the right content when you do not know who you are creating it for? If you ask most newbie bloggers who their target audience is, they will only give you a broad definition. For instance, if you ask a newbie automotive blogger who their target audience is, they might tell you that it is anyone who drives. However, this audience is too broad. Content written for a twenty-five-year-old chap who drives a high-powered sports car will not work for a sixty-five-year-old granny with her van. Similarly, the same content will not work for a middle-aged man who drives a truck.

Defining your target audience involves totally profiling and understanding them. Who are they? What is their average age? Where are they located? What are their likes and dislikes? Which challenges do they face the most? Where do they like hanging out online? Without answering these questions, it will be challenging to come up with content that is relevant to them. You will also have a huge problem trying to reach them.

So, how do you figure out who your target audience is? Luckily, there are several online resources that you can use to identify your target audience. For instance, you can use free survey tools like Google Forms or Survey Monkey to survey your site visitors. This will help you understand your audience, their pain points and what they expect from you.

You can also use web analytic and SEO tools to understand your audience. For instance, you can use Alexa to understand your competitors. This tool will help you gather information about their visitors, where they get most of their traffic from and which other blogs have a similar audience. Understanding your competitors' audience can give you fresh look on your blog. This tool will also help you to analyze your own visitors. Other similar web analytics/SEO tools that you can use include SpyFu, SEM Rush, and Similar Web. If you have multiple writers on your blog, you can use tools like Xtensio to create a reader persona. This is important for ensuring that all the writers clearly understand your target audience.

Mistake 2: Not Building An Email List From Day One

Most new bloggers focus on building their readership to significant levels before they start collecting readers' email addresses. I will use an example of my own experience to show you the importance of building an email list from day one. I had made the same mistake on one of my earliest blogs. Though I had built a significant readership for my blog, I did not have a huge email list. One morning, I woke up to find that I had lost over half of my traffic due to Google's first Penguin algorithm update. As you can expect, my income also took a hit.

If I had built an email list for my blog from day one, I would not have suffered this huge loss. Even with the update, I would have simply reached a huge chunk of my readers through email. You should not wait for an update to take you back to square one the way I did. Start collecting your visitors' email addresses immediately.

The problem with most bloggers is that they worry that asking visitors for their email addresses will bother them and push them away from the blog. If you do it the right way, you have nothing to worry about. Here are some pointers on how to collect emails the right way:

Offer freebies and content upgrades: One good way of getting your visitors to willingly share their email addresses is to offer content upgrades and freebies that are only accessible through your email newsletter. These freebies could be things like email courses, eBooks, podcasts, and so on. A great way of doing this is to create a great blog posts that helps your readers address some of their most pertinent needs. At the end of the post, let the readers know that you have another piece of content that covers the topic in greater detail, and then let them know that this content is available for free to your email subscribers. This should be followed by a subscription form where they can sign up to your email list.

Use an effective Call-To-Action (CTA): One mistake that most bloggers make is that they create content and then leave it at that. Your visitors have read your content, now what? You need to tell them what you need them to do. This is where a CTA comes in. It spurs them to take action. The most effective CTAs are clear and to the point. Let the reader know what they stand to gain by subscribing to your email list. If possible, create a sense of urgency to spur them to take action immediately. You should also place your CTA strategically to ensure that it gets the most results. For instance, instead of placing it at the end of your post (many readers don't make it to the end), you can place it in the middle of the post or on the side of the page.

Use media-rich content: If you want people to share their email address, you should always create content that gets them eager to hear again from you. Rather than simply sharing walls of text on your posts, intersperse it with images and videos to break the monotony of reading and keep the readers engaged.

Mistake 3: Not Promoting Your Posts Aggressively

In Chapter Six, I noted that content may be king, but promotion is queen. Great content can only get you so far. If people do not find and read your great content, then it doesn't really serve any purpose. Some things you should do to promote your posts include:

Notify your email subscribers: Earlier, I talked about the importance of collecting your readers' email addresses. Every time you put up a new post, you should notify your subscribers that you have a new post up on the blog.

Notify your guests: If you post contains quotes by other bloggers or links to posts by other bloggers, you should let these bloggers know that you have quoted them or linked to them. Ask them to share your content with their readers. Most will have no problem doing this, and it will be a win-win situation for both of you.

Share on social media: This should come as a no-brainer. Every time you post something new on your blog, you should share it on all your social media channels.

Use Facebook Ads: Facebook ads are a great way of driving paid traffic to your blog. This is because getting started is easy, they are relatively cheap, they offer very excellent audience targeting and they are effective in almost every niche.

Mistake 4: Using Too Many Banners And Popups

Popups are a great way of selling a product or converting visitors into subscribers. Many bloggers have seen great results from using popups within their blogs. So, naturally, you will be inclined to use popups on your blog as well, right? Of course, if something works, it makes sense to use it. The problem is that owing to their high conversion rates, popups have become overused, to the extent that they are negatively affecting user experience.

For a moment, consider your average reader. They probably visit lots of websites every day. Now imagine encountering a popup in each of the websites they visit. This can quickly become annoying. To make matters worse, some bloggers bombard visitors with popups that are irrelevant to them. This can lead to visitors making a quick exit any time they encounter a pop up. Actually, data shows that irrelevant popups annoy about 70% of American internet users.

To deal with the menace of popups, Google announced in January 2017 that it will begin cracking down on websites with intrusive advertisements (which is where popups fall). Therefore, to avoid pushing away your visitors as well as to keep in line with Google's recommendations, you should only use popups in moderation, and ensure that you are only using those that are relevant to your average audience.

Mistake 5: Going It Solo

Another huge mistake most beginners make is to think that blogging should be a one man show. The good news is, you don't have to do everything by yourself. It is much easier to achieve success when you have other good people helping you and some great resources to make things easier. If you decide to go it solo, there is a high chance you will face burnout, thereby limiting your blog's ability to grow. Putting in too many hours and trying to do everything by yourself will only make you less efficient and less effective over time. To avoid stifling your blog's growth by trying to do everything, you should find freelancers and outsource some of your tasks to them. There are several freelancing sites where you can find professional freelancers to help you with most of your blogging tasks.

Mistake 6: Not Developing Your Blog After Launch

After launching their blogs, some bloggers neglect everything else and only focus on creating content. This is a mistake that might cost you some traffic. Visitors to your site will notice that your blog is rarely updated, and they might just conclude that your products and services are not so relevant, either. You should keep in mind that blog development is a continuous process. There are always improvements to be made to make your blog faster, to make it look better or to present your content better. You should constantly keep finding ways of improving your blog's user experience.

Mistake 7: Forgetting About SEO

If you ask experienced internet marketers, they will tell you that creating content solely for SEO purposes is a proven way to push away readers from your blog post. However, you need to keep in mind that the opposite is also true. You should not completely ignore SEO if you want to take advantage of search traffic. Unfortunately, this is what most new bloggers do. They create content without bothering about the SEO aspects of the content. They do not do any keyword research or find other ways of improving their SEO. Sure, SEO is difficult, with search engines changing their search algorithms every now and then. However, you should not make the mistake of totally ignoring SEO. Search engines are still one of the major sources of traffic for most blogs; therefore, you should put some effort into ensuring that you capture some of this traffic.

Mistake 8: Expecting To Go From 0 To 10K Readers Overnight

If you visit blogging groups on Facebook, you will come across new bloggers complaining that they have only 100 views on their blog yet they have been consistently blogging for a month. Here's the kicker: that is to be expected! Actually, if you started blogging a month ago, 100 views shows that you are on the right track. Instead of complaining and feeling discouraged, you should be rejoicing. The problem with newbie bloggers is that they compare themselves with established bloggers who receive thousands of views per day, not knowing that these bloggers started the same way.

Building a successful blog takes time. If you go into it expecting to be an overnight success, you will be disappointed and discouraged. This is the reason why most newbie bloggers give up. After a few months of blogging without any significant traffic, they see themselves as having failed and throw in the towel. However, if you exercise some patience, your blog will definitely grow.

Now, you should be ready to go. If you take care to avoid these mistakes, you will already be ahead of most other newbie bloggers. You will save yourself a lot of time, money, and resources. However, if you make a mistake, don't be discouraged. Instead, learn from it and grow!

Chapter Summary

- You need to define your target audience to be able to produce the right content for them.
- You should start collecting your visitors' email addresses immediately after you launch your blog.
- You should promote aggressively every time you put up a new post.
- You should avoid using banners ad popups excessively. If you do use them, you should only use them in moderation, and ensure that you are only using those that are relevant to your average audience.
- Don't go solo. Instead, delegate and outsource some tasks.
- Do not ignore SEO.

Be patient. Don't expect to go from 0 to 10,000 readers overnight. Success takes time.

Final Words

This book has provided you with all the information you need to build your own blog from scratch and turn it into a money-making machine capable of bringing in over $100,000 on a regular basis. I have taught you how to pick the right niche, how to come up with the perfect name for your blog, how to set up your blog, how to come up with a content strategy, how to drive traffic to your blog and the numerous ways through which you can turn your blog into a money-making machine. I have also given you a list of the most common mistakes that you should avoid when launching your blog.

All you need now is to go out, put the information in this book to use, and start building your blog. One thing I will tell is that it is not a simple task. You will need to invest a lot of your time and effort. You need to be disciplined and stick to your content schedule. You need to get aggressive at promoting your content. However, if you do everything right, I can promise that your blog will definitely become a money maker. Now is the time to take action. Start working on your blog today!

Finally, I would really appreciate it if you leave your honest review for this book. It will only take a minute, and it will go a long way in helping me continue producing such high-quality books for you.

I wish you all the best as you start your blogging career!

www.ingramcontent.com/pod-product-compliance
Lightning Source LLC
Chambersburg PA
CBHW070146230526
45471CB00002B/545